Word Bird's

No! No! Word Bird

Published in the United States of America by The Child's World®, Inc.
PO Box 326
Chanhassen, MN 55317-0326
800-599-READ
www.childsworld.com

Project Manager Mary Berendes
Editor Katherine Stevenson, Ph.D.
Designer Ian Butterworth

Library of Congress Cataloging-in-Publication Data
Moncure, Jane Belk.
No! no! Word Bird / by Jane Belk Moncure.
p. cm.
Summary: Word Bird experiences hot soup, cold snow,
and wet clothes on a snowy winter day.
ISBN 1-56766-991-3 (lib. : alk. paper)
[1. Winter—Fiction. 2. Birds—Fiction.]   I. Title.
PZ7.M739 No 2002
[E]—dc21
2001006058

Word Bird's™

No! No! Word Bird

by Jane Belk Moncure

illustrated by Chris McEwan

"No! No!" said Mama.
"The stove is hot!"

"Hot! Yes, hot!"

"No! No!" said Mama.
"The snow is cold!"

"Cold! Yes, cold!"

"Come back!" said Mama.
"The snow is cold!"

"Wear your cap,

your scarf,

and your boots."

"No! No!" said Mama.
"Come down!"

"Oh no!"

"No! No!" said Mama.
"Take off your cap,…

and your scarf,

and your boots.

You are wet!"

"Yes, I am wet and cold," said Word Bird.

"Come here," said Mama.
"The fire is hot."

"The soup is hot,"
said Mama.

"I am hot," said Word
Bird. "I am dry. I am
going out. Bye-bye."

"No! No!" said Mama.
"Come back! The snow
is cold!"

"Wear your cap,

your scarf,

and your boots."

"Hi, friends,"
said Word Bird.

"Hi, Word Bird!
Let's go for a ride."

"No! No!" said Mama.
"You will fall off!"

"Oh no!"

"Let's skate,"
said Word Bird.

"We can race. Go!"

"No! No!" said Mama.
"Come back!"

"No! No!" said Word Bird.
"Come back!"

"Good! You are a
good bird," said Mama.

"Yes. I am a good bird."

Can you read these words with Word Bird?

bird

no

stove

hot

snow

cold

cap

scarf

boots

wet

fire

soup

out

ride

skate

race

yes